Table of Contents

Getting Started

An introduction and how to use this book

What's this book about? How can it help me?

This book contains all our analytics, conclusions and lessons from analyzing the largest sample of exam results collected outside of CFA Institute.

There's a lot to learn from thousands of past experiences. Difficult topics, passing scores, an assessment of how competitive the field is, the importance of your work and education background – these are just a few things you will learn from this book.

> *The Minimum Passing Score (MPS) is the score you have to beat to pass your CFA exam.*

So what's this Minimum Passing Score that you talk about?

In simple terms, the Minimum Passing Score (MPS) is the score you have to beat to pass your CFA exam. This normally is around the 55%-70% range. Do not confuse this with the *pass rate*, which is normally lower and represents the percentage of candidates that passed a particular exam.

CFA Institute strongly feels that the MPS should not be a focus of the exams as it leads to unfair comparisons across years. Consequently CFA Institute has never made any MPS for any level public.

In earlier days, the MPS was a simple formula - 70% of the highest scoring candidate for that year. If the highest-scoring candidate scored 90%, the MPS would therefore be 70%*90% = 63%. Some candidates still mistakenly believe that this is the method used to determine the MPS today.

Presently, the MPS is determined by a custom methodology devised by CFA

Institute, and one of the primary inputs is a series of workshops based on the Angoff model. A large, diverse group of CFA charterholders evaluate the entire exam individually question by question and makes a judgment on the performance of the just-competent candidate. In other words, envisioning a candidate they judge to be just good enough to pass, they estimate the probability that this candidate will get this question right.

> *One of the primary inputs (into the MPS) is a series of workshops based on the Angoff model.*

Once all the evaluations are done, the charterholders take a look at actual candidate performance and the evaluation process is repeated again. Psychometricians oversee the entire process and the results of this workshop is the main reference (but not the final word) for setting the MPS.

The CFA Institute Board of Governors then puts all information on the table. All available information is considered including recommendations from the Angoff workshop (which is the most important input), and then a final decision is made on the MPS. The objective is to set a consistent competency level across years.

You therefore pass by being better than what CFA Institute defines as a 'just-competent' candidate. This may be indirectly influenced by the performance of candidates taking the same exam as you, but it definitely is not a primary driver. So remarks such as 'bringing down the curve' are not exactly accurate.

So I should aim for a score similar to the MPS then?

No. In short, always aim to beat 70%. Always, always, always.

The MPS calculations in this book are for your reference, and to see how this has changed over the years. Aiming to just beat the MPS is still terrible practice. No matter what information is disclosed on the MPS, with the exam format as it stands, you should always aim for 70% and above. Difficulties change across papers and years as well.

If you aim to be just good enough, all it takes to be burned is one or two slips, or for the bar to be raised slightly.

> *Your actual score is not released by the CFA Institute. Exam results will be emailed to you and topics will receive 'grades' in 3 categories.*

Where's my actual score? What do the score categories mean?

Your actual score is not released by CFA Institute. Don't ask us why; we don't know either.

Exam results will be emailed to you and topics will receive 'grades' in 3 categories:

- **Poor** – less or equal to 50%
- **Poor to average** - between 50% and 70%
- **Above average** - more than 70%

A typical exam's results email may look like this. This is an actual email from one of us in the 300 Hours team, with some details changed:

Dear So and So,

Congratulations. I am very pleased to inform you that you passed the June 20XX Level III CFA exam. You are one step closer to achieving your goal of earning the globally respected CFA charter.

XX% of candidates passed the June 20XX Level III CFA exam. Your detailed exam results, including a matrix outlining your strengths and weaknesses, are in the table below.

Now that you have passed Level III, you must be a regular member of CFA Institute to be eligible for the award of the CFA charter. Log in now to verify your current membership status or complete the application process.

Again, congratulations on your achievement.

Sincerely,

John D. Rogers, CFA

President and Chief Executive Officer

CFA Institute

The three columns on the right are marked with asterisks to indicate your performance on each topic area.

Essay

Q#	Topic	Max Pts	<=50%	51%-70%	>70%
1	Portfolio Management - Individual	15	*	-	-
2	Portfolio Management - Individual	23	*	-	-
3	Portfolio Management - Institutional	26	-	*	-
4	Economics	23	-	-	*
5	Portfolio Management - Asset Allocation	20	*	-	-
6	Fixed Income Investments	19	-	*	-
7	Equity Investments	22	-	*	-
8	Portfolio Management - Risk Management	16	-	-	*
9	Portfolio Management – Performance Eval.	16	*	-	-

Item-Set

Q#	Topic	Max Pts	<=50%	51%-70%	>70%
-	Alternative Investments	18	-	*	-
-	Economics	18	-	*	-
-	Equity Investments	18	-	*	-
-	Ethical & Professional Standards	36	-	-	*
-	Fixed Income Investments	36	-	-	*
-	Portfolio Management - Execution	18	-	-	*
-	Portfolio Management - Individual	18	-	-	*
-	Portfolio Management - Risk Management	18	-	-	*

As you see you get an indication of what range you scored in for each category, but not your exact score. If you'd like more insight as to what the implications of your results are, that's what our Analyze Results section (go.300hours.com/results) is for.

Pass rates are low because they're counting all the people that didn't show up. Right?

Wrong. No-shows are excluded from the official pass rates.

No-shows are not counted in the official pass rates.

Pass rates for the CFA exam are not great - usually coming in at <= 50% especially at the lower levels. They however do not include candidates that were absent on exam day, who are about 25% of all registered candidates every year. So if you were thinking to yourself that the pass rates are low because loads of people weren't serious about it and didn't show, that's just not true, unfortunately.

I entered my score into go.300hours.com/results. What do the calculated maximum, minimum and 40/60/80 scores mean?

This is a bit of a long one. But see if you can follow us through this.

As your score comes in three categories with a corresponding points range, there are several simple assumptions we can make about this. This is best illustrated using a table:

Simple view:

Score category	<=50%	51%-70%	>70%
Minimum score	0%	51%	71%
Maximum score	50%	70%	100%

40/60/80 score   40%   60%   80%

This is the easiest way to understand how the various sets of scores are defined and calculated.

In practice, however, we at 300 Hours have taken this to a more detailed level. There are further implications depending on the format of the exam of what actually can be the possibilities of the minimum, maximum and 40/60/80 scores.

Let's take the first category of the Item-Set portion of the Level III score in the sample email, Alternative Investments, as an example. The 'max points' for this category is 18, which means that this was a 6 question item-set (6 questions at 3 points each).

The actual assumptions that should be made for a more accurate calculation should therefore be as the following table. Note that many numbers for the minimum and maximum assumptions are now different compared to the simple view above.

Accurate view (for Alt Investments, six questions, Level III example):

Score category	<=50%	51%-70%	>70%
Minimum score	0/6 = 0%	4/6 = 66%	5/6 = 83%
Maximum score	3/6 = 50%	4/6 = 66%	6/6 = 100%
40/60/80 score	40%	60%	80%

If this category had 12 questions, such as Ethics in the example above, the scores change again.

Accurate view (for Ethics, 12 questions, Level III example):

Score category	<=50%	51%-70%	>70%
Minimum score	0/12 = 0%	7/12 = 58%	9/12 = 75%
Maximum score	6/12 = 50%	8/12 = 67%	12/12 = 100%
40/60/80 score	40%	60%	80%

All our analyses use the accurate view generated for our calculations for each individual category, each individual level, each individual exam year. A lot of work? You bet it is.

This is also why you may find small differences if you use the 'simple' set of assumptions.

What do the 'bands' mean?

In your results email, you will receive a pass / fail grade. In the case of a Fail, you also get an additional Band 1-10 score. Band scores divide all failing candidates for that particular exam into 10 categories, with Band 1 being the furthest away from a pass, and Band 10 being the closest to passing.

> *Band scores divide all failing candidates into 10 categories, with Band 10 being closest to a pass.*

The differences between bands are not made public, but they are naturally a function of how close the distribution of scores of failing candidates are. For our analyses we also always include an assessment of how close these band differences were for each exam. This will give a better indicator for failing candidates as to exactly how far from passing they got to this time (in terms of % or number of questions).

Section 1: What are the topics that matter in each CFA exam level?

Introduction

So what makes a particular CFA topic 'matter'?

It's a difficult question to answer at first, and of course the traditional answer should be that 'they all matter'. But from a pure pass-the-exam perspective, some topics do matter more than others.

We've identified three reasons why candidates should pay attention to a particular topic:

*   Because it has a **significant weighting** in the CFA exam
*   Because usually candidates find it **challenging to obtain a high score**
*   Because **it's Ethics** (see the "Note on Ethics" in the following section).

> *From a pure pass-the-exam perspective, some topics do matter more than others.*

We've used these guiding principles above to distil the key areas that each CFA candidate should be focusing their attention to. Follow them well, and you'll optimize your preparation for the CFA exams.

What you will learn in this section:

*   Which topics matter to your specific CFA Level
*   Which topics do candidates perform well or poorly
*   Our recommendations on how to group and approach these topics

A Note on Ethics

Ethics is an important subject matter for several reasons:

Highly Transferable Knowledge

Ethics is 15% of Level I, and 10% of Level II and III. Although not the largest section, the topics and LOS statements on Ethics are very similar across all levels. This means that the information you retain in Level I will still be exactly applicable in Level III questions. Combine that with the relatively little amount of time needed to master Ethics and suddenly you have a very effort-efficient topic in your hands. Be a master of Ethics in Level I, and you'll see benefits throughout the subsequent levels.

The "Ethics Adjustment"

Besides its transferable knowledge across levels, Ethics is also unique in a very important way. The CFA Institute implements a factor called the 'ethics adjustment' for candidates within the passing score. Taken from the CFA website:

*"The Board of Governors instituted a policy to place particular emphasis on ethics. **Starting with the 1996 exams, the performance on the ethics section became a factor in the pass/fail decision for candidates whose total scores bordered the minimum passing score. The ethics adjustment can have a positive or negative impact on these candidates' final results."***

This means that if you're a borderline fail, you can be lifted into the passing zone by a strong performance in Ethics. Similarly, if you were a borderline pass, you could be failed if your Ethics performance was particularly weak.

However, the CFA Institute has stated that you're more likely to be 'passed' through ethics adjustment than 'failed'.

Level I topic analysis

The three following charts show how candidates have done across topics in the most recent 4 Level I exams (Dec 12, Jun 13, Dec 13, Jun 14). In general, performance by topic has been steady across exams in the past 3 years.

Topic-by-topic breakdown: All candidates in sample

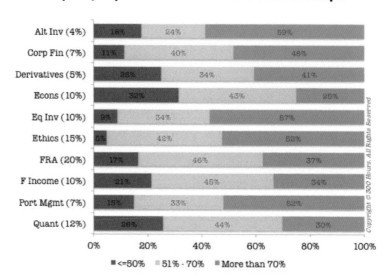

Performance by topic has been steady across exams in the past 3 years.

Topic-by-topic breakdown: Passing candidates in sample

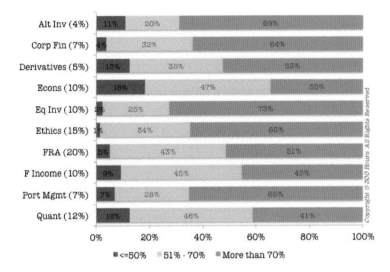

Topic-by-topic breakdown: Failing candidates in sample

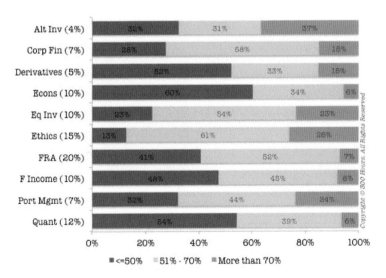

After iterations of discussions and analyzing each topic, we found that the most useful view was through 3 tiers or approximately increasing difficulty:

- **Tier 1: Basic**. These are the subjects where candidates tend to do well in. This includes Ethics, which is an extremely important topic and is shown by the candidates' performance, and Equity Investments.

- **Tier 2: Advanced**. Some topics, such as Alternative Investments and Portfolio management, can be polarizing. What this means is that there is a high percentage of candidates that do very well or very badly, with little in between. Take the time to understand the underlying principles behind these topics. The other topics in Tier 2 are Corporate Finance, FRA and Fixed Income.

- **Tier 3: Tough**. These are the difficult and often heavy-weighted topics: Derivatives, Economics and Quantitative Methods. Take care to pay attention to these topics from the start.

Each individual topic is outlined in the table below. Use this table as your guiding principle to approaching your topics in Level I.

Level I topics can be grouped into 3 tiers: Basic, Advanced, and Tough

The least you need to know:

Tier	Topic	% weighting	Recommendations
Basic	Ethics	15%	Key topic areas. Master them early in Level I to pay dividends later at every level.
	Equity Investments	10%	
Advanced	Alternative Investments	4%	Alt Inv and Portfolio Management are highly polarizing - either candidates get it, or they do badly in it.
	Corporate Finance	7%	
	FRA	20%	
	Fixed Income	10%	Invest in the time to understand the subject matter - rote memorisation will not be of much help.
	Portfolio Management	7%	
Tough	Derivatives	5%	Derivatives questions can be some of the trickiest
	Economics	10%	

Quantitative Methods	12%	you'll encounter in Level I. Quant Methods is a challenging topic, but highly important as it underpins a significant amount of the CFA material.

Level II topic analysis

In general, strong and weak areas are less distinct compared to Level I - the differences between candidates seem to have diminished in Level II. The data below is from the past 3 Level II exams (2012, 2013, 2014)

Topic-by-topic breakdown: All candidates in sample

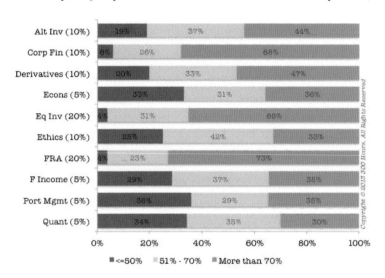

Strong and weak areas are less distinct in Level II compared to Level I.

Topic-by-topic breakdown: Passing candidates in sample

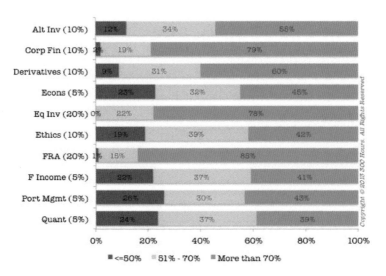

Topic-by-topic breakdown: Failing candidates in sample

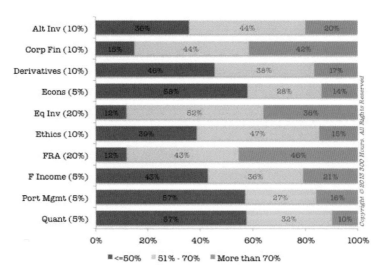

We've not grouped topics by difficulty for Level II. Instead, we've split the topics into 2 main groups: Heavyweights, and Others.

Heavyweights (total weighting 60%)

- Corporate Finance
- Equity Investments
- Ethics
- FRA

Heavyweight topics are incredibly important for Level II.

Heavyweights are incredibly important for Level II, for 2 simple reasons:

- Together, they are responsible for a whopping 60% of the exam
- These are topics where the passing and failing candidates differ the most in performance

What does this mean? Make sure that you hit these topics with everything you've got, and prioritize these until you've gotten them mastered.

The least you need to know:

Tier	Topic	% weight	Recommendations
Heavyweights	Corporate Finance	10%	There is a large difference between passing and failing candidates in these topics. Make sure you've mastered these topics when you approach the
	FRA	20%	
	Equity Investments	20%	

	Ethics	10%	Level II exam. Ethics again is key especially with Ethics adjustments. For more information on the Ethics adjustment, see 'A Note on Ethics' at the start of this section.
Others	Alternative Investments	10%	
	Derivatives	10%	
	Economics	5%	Derivatives, Alt Inv and Fixed Income questions can be devilishly tricky – practice is key.
	Fixed Income	5%	
	Portfolio Management	5%	
	Quantitative Methods	5%	

Level III topic analysis

Level III sets a significantly different trend compared to the previous 2 levels, so we've taken a different approach to this section compared to the previous levels.

> *The essay format is one of the largest factors in passing or failing CFA Level III.*

The essay format, a.k.a. one of the largest factors in passing or failing Level III. The largest curveball in Level III is the constructed response format, better known as the essay format paper in the morning session. Get to know the format early in your Level III preparation as this will have a significant influence on your chances of passing.

Knowing that this is a very important factor, we spoke to Level III respondents of our survey that did exceptionally well in the essay section, and asked them to share their own preparation and test-taking tips. The detailed lessons from this can be found later in this book in Section 7.

Instead of focusing on the performance on candidates by topics and questions, the most useful analysis we carried out for Level III is a breakdown of topics by weighting and format for the past 3 years, as found in the following chart.

Level III 2011-2013 topics by weighting and question format

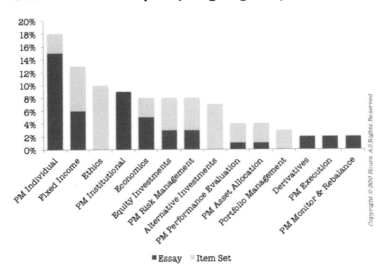

■ Essay　░ Item Set

Not all topics are created equal. Individual Portfolio Management, including Behavioural Finance and IPS (Investment Policy Statement), has consistently been the highest-weighted topic for Level III in the past 3 years.

Topics are not represented equally in the essay or item-set format. When revising topics for Level III, it is also key to understand which format (item set vs essay) the topic is likely to be tested in. Some topics such as PM Individual, PM Institutional and Derivatives are often concentrated in the essay paper, whereas topics such as Ethics and Alternative Investments typically are found in the item-set paper.

The least you need to know:

- Make sure you focus on Individual Portfolio Management and IPS-type questions. (A great IPS discussion on the 300 Hours forum can be read at go.300hours.com/sophieips)

- Ensure that you know what format (item-set vs essay) that each topic is likely to be tested in and practice accordingly.

- Get familiar with the essay format as early on in your exam prep as possible.

Not all topics are the same in Level III, both in weighting and format.

Section 2: How large are the differences between failing bands?

Level I failing bands

If you failed a CFA exam at some point, you might have wondered exactly did your failing band mean. How far were you from passing?

> *The average difference between Level I failing bands is about 9 questions.*

From observing the Level I data across 2012 to 2014, the average percentage difference between bands is about 4%, or about 9 questions in the Level I exam. This means that if you got a Band 7, you were on average 9 more correct questions away from being in the same point in Band 8.

We've now collected data across 4 different Level I exams – results have been consistent across exams. The chart for Level I band differences is shown below.

Level 1 band difference: 3.8%, or about 9 questions between bands

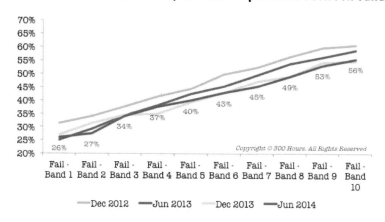

Level II failing bands

The percentage differences between failing bands are much smaller compared with Level I. For Level I, the difference between bands was about 9 questions. In Level II, the difference between bands is only about 3.5%, or 4 questions.

This means that assuming you were around the mid-point of your band, you were just a few questions away from reaching the next band.

Level 2 band difference: 3.5%, or about 4 item set questions

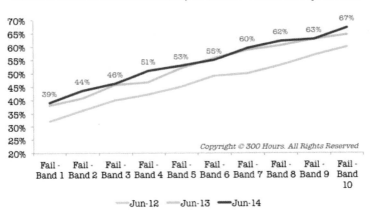

Why do so few questions separate the bands compared to Level I? Two reasons:

Reason #1: Competition is fiercer. The variation of quality between Level II candidates is also much lower compared to Level I. Remember, all Level II candidates would have already passed Level I, so the more casual candidates would have been weeded out already.

Since the bands are defined in relative terms (e.g. Band 10 meant you are in the top 10% of failing candidates and so on) this would mean the differences in bands would be much smaller. We see this intensify further in the Level III analysis.

Reason #2: Less questions, therefore worth more points. There are less questions in Level II compared to Level I (half, actually), so even if the percentage differences remain the same, the number of questions between bands would be halved.

Fiercer competition and less questions lead to a closer failing band difference in Level II.

Questions are worth more, so pay closer attention.

Level III failing bands

The band differences continue to establish the Level III exam as competitive. Very competitive.

> The differences in Level III failing bands are very, very close: 1.7% on average.

The differences in bands are very, very close in Level III. Just 1.57% on average separates each band, which is the equivalent of 1-2 questions in the item-set, or 6 essay points. That's the difference that could push you from Band 9 to Band 10, and so on.

The competition is obviously the hottest at Level III. At the last level, there are very few 'casual candidates'. These guys are nearly at the peak of Everest, so they're going to plant the flag, or die trying. That's probably why there is such a small difference between bands (and passing/failing).

The following graph shows the band difference estimation for Level III illustrated by the dark blue line (2013) and the grey line (2012).

Level 3 band difference: 1.7%, about 2 item set questions or 6 essay points

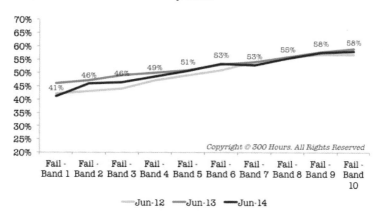

We can see (perhaps expectedly) the band differences become smaller and smaller as we progress up the levels. This is shown in the following chart – note that the slopes of the line graphs decrease with each level, indicating a smaller difference across failing bands.

2012-2014 average exam band differences: Levels I, II, III

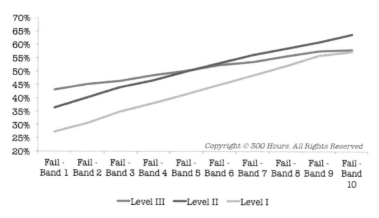

The Level II line, while not significantly decreased in gradient compared to

Level I, is significantly higher. This shows the increased level of difficulty in the Level II exam compared to Level I. The sharp decrease in gradient in the Level III line again highlights how close-scoring candidates are in the Level III exam.

CFA failing bands on the whole are set incredibly close. Quite often, just one or two questions separate you from the next band. So if you've failed, take comfort in the fact that you're likely to have been much closer to passing than you'd probably thought based on your failing band.

Quite often, just one or two questions separate you from the next band.

Section 3: What is the estimated Minimum Passing Score?

Introduction, and a few important points

Before we dive into the details - a very important reminder to you, as a candidate. Do not use the Minimum Passing Score (MPS) as a benchmark

The MPS numbers in this section are from our deductive analysis, not the CFA Institute.

to aim for in your prep. Aim to beat 70%, not the MPS. For more information, see the "Getting Started" section.

Another very important point - the MPS numbers we talk about here are from our deductive analysis and is in no way endorsed by the CFA Institute. The CFA Institute does NOT release MPS figures (which is the point of our analysis in the first place) so if you've got questions about the MPS estimates in this guide, do get in touch with us, not the CFA Institute!

What you will learn in this section:

- A base idea of how challenging the actual exam will be based on our estimated MPS levels
- How the estimated MPS has trended over the past years
- How the MPS changes across CFA levels

The MPS vs 'pass rates'

The MPS, as detailed in the introduction of this guide, is the minimum score determined at each CFA exam to be given a pass. Beat the MPS, and you pass. The MPS is never officially released by the CFA Institute and varies across levels and years.

The pass rate is the percentage of passing candidates of all attending candidates for any given CFA exam. This rate, on the other hand, is released every year by the CFA Institute on results day and is notoriously low.

In this section we'll refer to both MPS and pass rates in our tips and recommendations - make sure you know the difference!

Estimating the MPS

The following chart shows how an estimate for the MPS can be calculated. The chart shows a visual representation of every candidate submission in a particular exam and year, as a single green (passing candidate) or red (failing candidate) vertical line. The top of the lines are the maximum possible scores for each candidate, and the bottom of each line are the minimum possible scores.

> *MPS and pass rates are not the same thing — make sure you know the difference!*

Triangulating maximum, minimum and pass/fail grades gives us a range of possibilities where the MPS could lie. Given enough data points and enough performance difference between candidates, we can deduce what the MPS is.

Estimating the MPS example – passing and failing candidates

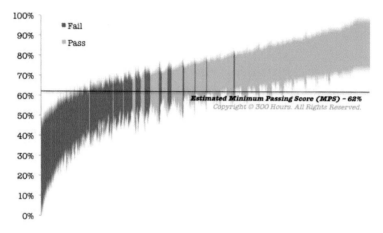

Level I MPS analysis

This edition, we've collected quite a few data points for the CFA Level I exam to be able to look at trends in the past few years. The estimated Minimum Passing Scores for the past five Level I exams are as below, compared alongside their published pass rates. Remember, MPS is the score needed to pass, and the pass rate is the percentage of candidates that passed that exam out of those who attended.

Level I estimated MPS and pass rates, Jun 2012 to Jun 2014

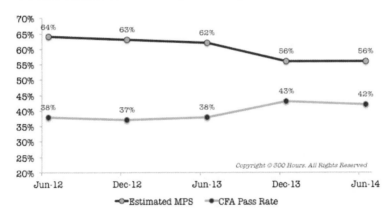

There is a clear inverse correlation between our estimated MPS and official pass rates. This is not unexpected – lowering the MPS makes it easier for candidate to pass.

In the past two Level I exams (Dec 2013 and Jun 2014), the estimated MPS has dropped a fair bit compared to the previous three exams (Jun 2012 to Jun 2013).

However, to be assured of a pass, we would still strongly recommend that you aim to exceed a score of 70% when attempting practice exams to have a reasonable chance of passing. The actual exam MPS is unlikely to exceed 70% in any given year.

The least you need to know:

- *MPS estimates for Level I are around 56-64% in the past 3 years*
- *However you should aim for >70% in practice exams*

The estimated MPS has been declining over recent years, inversely trending with official pass rates.

Level II MPS analysis

Level II estimated MPS and pass rates, Jun 2012 to Jun 2014

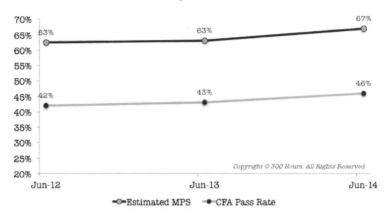

The Level II MPS levels average higher than Level I. This means that not only is it generally a more difficult exam due to the wide variety of topics covered, but it also usually requires a higher score to pass.

This reinforces advice that Level II is significantly more difficult than Level I. If you're a new Level I candidate, do not assume that Level II will be a similar experience to Level I. Prepare harder, and aim higher.

The estimated MPS has been fairly steady, but has increased slightly in the past year, alongside the passing score. This may suggest that the standard of the average Level II candidate has increased.

The *least you need to know*:

- *MPS estimates for Level II are around 63-67% in the past 3 years*
- *This is a higher and more tightly clustered range than Level I – meaning more consistently challenging!*

Level III MPS analysis

Level III estimated MPS and pass rates, Jun 2012 to Jun 2014

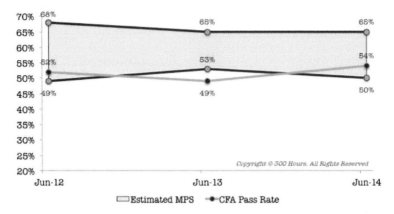

Level III Minimum Passing Scores are a lot more difficult to estimate.

The reason for this is that the constructed response AM section format and results categories yields a wider range of minimums and maximums for each submission, making it significantly more difficult to estimate an exact MPS.

Another reason contributing to the difficulty in estimating the Level III MPS is that the standard between passing and failing Level III candidates are very close. For more evidence on the close performance levels between passing and failing Level III candidates, see section 2.

Hence in the Level III section we've presented our MPS estimates in the form of ranges. The deduced ranges of the Level III MPS for the past 3 years is shown in the following chart.

For the Level III MPS estimates, as with the Level II estimates we were able to deduce a more accurate range for 2013 compared to 2012, with an increased sample size. The 2013 Level III MPS was deduced to be in the range of 53-65%.

The Level III MPS is lower than the MPS for Level I & II.

The upper part of the range for the Level III MPS estimates have been in the range of 65-68%, which really emphasizes the need to maintain a high score in your practice exams to maximize your pass chances.

However a significant issue for almost all candidates is the morning constructed response paper, better known as the 'essay' paper. More information on how to approach the essay paper can be found in Section 7.

The least you need to know:

- *Level III MPS scores are difficult to estimate, but the upper ranges are fairly close to 70%*
- *Candidate competition is fierce at this point*
- *The essay section has to be mastered to pass, and cannot be ignored*

Section 4: When should I start my CFA study preparation?

Introduction

In our CFA Results Analysis (go.300hours.com/analyze) we include an optional question in our research, asking candidates for the month they started their CFA studies.

By including this question, we can better learn how early preparation can influence pass rates, and therefore better inform future candidates on when is the best time to start preparing. We've also cross-analyzed responses with results to investigate if there is a correlation between start times and exam performance.

What you will learn in this section:

- When are the most popular start times for CFA candidates
- How start times vary across CFA levels
- Our recommendations on when to start for each level

We investigate when the majority of candidates start their CFA prep and how this varies across exam results.

Level I

The following chart shows the candidate samples for the Level I exam by the month that they started their CFA preparations respectively, across December and June exams in 2013 and 2014.

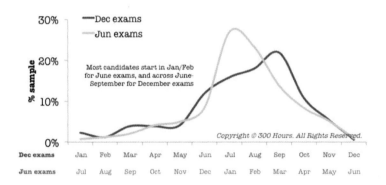

Level I study start months, 2013-2014

From the chart, it's clear that the majority of candidates start their studies in January or February for the June exams, directly after the December holiday period. This gives an average of 4-5 months of study for the June exam: on 300Hours.com we recommend our readers to start after December for the June exam.

For the December exam, start dates are more spread out. A sensible start month would be June or July, however the spread across June to September is probably due to summer holiday seasons in many countries.

There are small differences between passing and failing candidates, but on the whole they are negligible. Make sure you start on the early side of the sample, but starting early isn't a guarantee to pass, it's how you choose to spend your time that counts.

The least you need to know:

- *If taking the June exams, recommended start in January*
- *If December exams, recommended start in June / July, but holiday season tends to influence many candidates*
- *Starting earlier does not significantly influence pass rate chances*

Level II

The following chart shows the candidate samples for the Level II exam by the month that they started their CFA preparations respectively across the 2013 and 2014 exams.

The overall Level I candidate sample for the June exams 2013-2014 is also shown here for comparison.

Level II and Level I study start months, 2013-2014

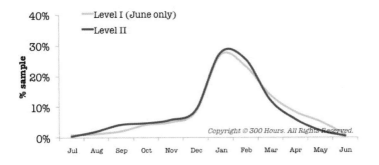

Again, a similar pattern to Level I is observed. A slightly higher proportion of Level II candidates now start in January and February compared to Level I. Again, there is almost no difference between passing and failing candidates, and Level II candidates start earlier on average compared to Level I. This difference is especially noticeable in the 'late' months (March to May).

Level II candidates start slightly earlier than Level I candidates.

The least you need to know:

- *The recommended start is still January, same as Level I June cycle*

- *More candidates now start in Jan-Feb rather than later*

- *Starting earlier does not significantly influence pass rate chances, however for Level II you will have to step up your effort in the same time period*

Level III

The next chart shows the 2013-2014 Level III candidate sample start months. The overall Level I & Level II candidate sample is also shown here for comparison.

Level III study start months with Level I and II comparison, 2013-2014

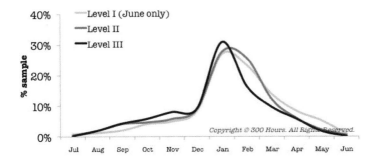

The trends we saw in Level II continue - Level III candidates start even earlier than Level I & II candidates, with the majority of them now having a strict start in January. There is also a significantly higher proportion of candidates starting in the year before.

This drives home our constant recommendation to our readers that starting early is key - many candidates underestimate how much material there is to go through, and by starting early you can get an early warning on this. Again, for the June exams we recommend that you start in early January, and June if you're taking the December Level I exams.

The least you need to know:

- *As you progress up the levels, the stricter you need to be with your start date*

- *January is by far the most popular start month for Level III*

- *Quite a few candidates start in Sep-Dec the previous year*

Section 5: How many practice exams should I aim for?

Introduction

Readers at 300Hours.com know that one of the most important aspects to preparation is setting aside enough time for practice exams. Completing as many practice papers as possible is one of the most sure-fire ways to improve your chances at passing.

But how many is enough? As charterholders, we know what worked for us, but is that really enough data to conclude? We asked the thousands of candidates that submitted their results to estimate how many mock and practice exams they attempted, to be able to provide solid recommendations for you.

What you will learn in this section:

- Average number of practice exams attempted by candidates across levels
- How the number of practice exams differ across CFA levels
- The correlation between the number of attempted practice exams and CFA exam performance
- The minimum number of practice exams you should be attempting for your exam

Average practice exams attempted, by grade & CFA level

From our analysis, it is very clear that CFA performance correlates strongly to the number of completed practice exams.

Another important observation is that the average number of practice papers completed also increases across Level I to III. The chart below shows the average number of practice papers attempted by grade across all CFA levels.

Practice papers completed by result, Level III, 2013-2014

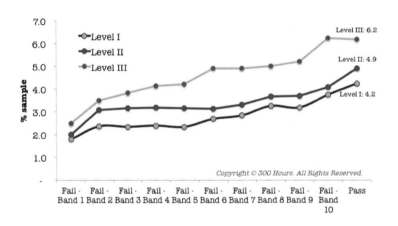

You can see that failing candidates consistently attempt less practice exams than passing candidates. Furthermore, there is a very clear correlation between the number of attempted practice exams and performance.

Level II candidates on the whole attempt nearly an entire extra practice exam compared to Level I candidates, and passing Level III candidates attempt more than 6 full AM and PM sessions. This corresponds with our research on the Level III essay paper in Section 7, where 'more practice exams' was overwhelmingly the dominant advice given.

Distribution of # practice papers

The first chart shows the distribution of practice papers completed for the June 2013 Level I candidate sample, with one practice paper defined as both AM and PM papers combined.

Distribution of # practice papers completed, Level I, 2013-2014

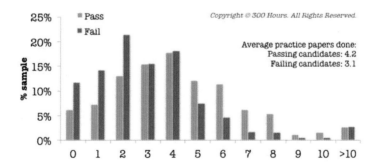

From the chart, there is a clear difference between passing and failing candidates. Passing candidates on average complete more practice papers than failing candidates: one whole practice paper extra on average.

59

Distribution of # practice papers completed, Level II, 2013-2014

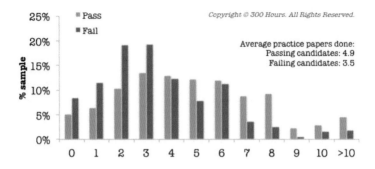

Distribution of # practice papers completed, Level III, 2013-2014

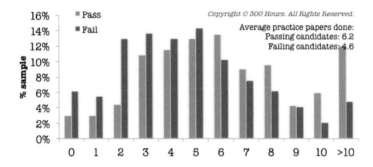

For Levels II and III, the same basic observation from Level I holds true - passing candidates on average completed one extra practice paper compared to failing candidates.

The quick lesson from this section and the previous section is therefore simple: to pass, start early and practice often, and increase your efforts even more with each CFA level. Use this guide to inform the minimum amount you should be aiming for.

The least you need to know:

- *Average practice exams completed by the passing candidate is about 4.2 for Level I, 4.9 in Level II and 6.2 in Level III*

- *Passing candidates consistently complete significantly more practice papers than failing candidates*

- *You should at least attempt 4 full practice exams for Level I, 5 for Level II and as many as you possibly can for Level III, especially for the essay session*

> *Passing candidates consistently complete more practice papers (4.2 in L1, 4.9 in L2, 6.2 in L3)*

Section 6: How important is having a background in finance?

Introduction

Knowledge of finance is useful, but the largest factor to failing the CFA exam is complacency.

Using our candidate results database, we can cross-reference exam performance with work and education backgrounds.

We asked candidates as they submitted their results whether their work and education background was finance related or otherwise. The results in this section will be able to inform current candidates if their background has any influence on their CFA exam performance – some conclusions can be quite unexpected!

What you will learn in this section:

- How does a background in finance influence CFA performance
- What candidate backgrounds perform poorly
- Our recommendations depending on your own background

In this analysis, we cross-reference exam performance with work and educational backgrounds.

The influence of a finance background in Level I

Sample by work and educational background, Level I

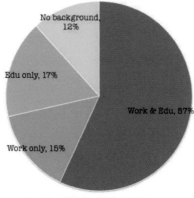

In our analysis, we then cross-referenced exam pass rates with these 4 background profiles:

- **Work & Edu**: those with financial backgrounds in both work and education

- **Work only**: those with financial background in work but not education

- **Edu only**: those with financial background in education but not work

- **No background**: no financial background in either work or education

4 background profiles were built across all CFA candidates.

The results were interesting and a bit unexpected: the following chart shows the result for the Level I candidates in December 2013 to June 2014

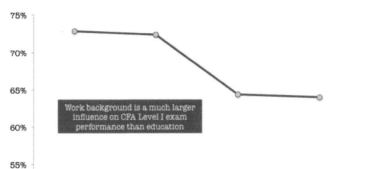

Pass Rate by Financial Background, Level I (2013-2014)

The group of candidates with both work and education backgrounds in finance are best-placed to do well in the CFA exams, followed by candidates with finance-related work, but a non-finance education.

This shows that work experience in finance is strongly relevant to good CFA performance. There are a few possibilities for this – candidates could be using financial knowledge gained at work in the exam, or have a stronger drive to perform better due to direct benefits from the CFA qualification.

Educational background surprisingly does not have much correlation to CFA performance. In fact, in June 2013, candidates with no work or educational finance backgrounds even outperformed those who had a finance education. This may be demonstrating a higher level of determination by candidates trying to break into finance.

There is no doubt that having some pre-education in finance helps CFA exam performance. In the case of the 'edu only' group, complacency may be the issue. Anecdotal feedback we've collected indicates that candidates with finance or economics degrees may tend to regard the CFA exams more lightly than other candidates. Additionally, without a work requirement to spur them on, candidates may find it difficult to maintain the drive and discipline necessary to complete their preparations properly.

The least you need to know:

- *Candidates with financial work experience tend to do well in Level I*
- *A financial educational background doesn't improve your CFA performance*
- *A financial background is far from a prerequisite for success in the CFA program*

The influence of a finance background in Level II

Sample by work and educational background, Level II (2013-2014)

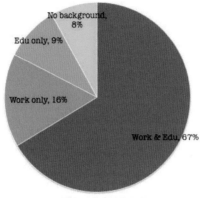

Pass Rate by Financial Background, Level II (2013-2014)

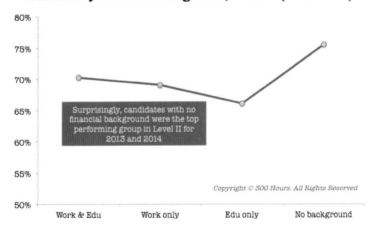

In Level II, not only did the group of candidates with no financial background outperform the candidates with financial education, but they were also the best-performing group of all. This result was consistent across the 2013 and

2014 exams. However, it is challenging to definitively find out why exactly do candidates with no financial background do well in Level II.

The groups with finance-related work experience were still high performing. The group with only finance-related education were the lowest-performing group.

The least you need to know:

- *Candidates with no financial background were the best performers in Level II for 2013 and 2014*
- *Financial work experience is still a strong contributing factor to performance in Level II*

No-background candidates were the best performers in Level II.

The influence of a finance background in Level III

Sample by work and educational background, Level III (2013-2014)

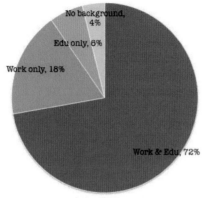

Pass Rate by Financial Background, Level III (2013-2014)

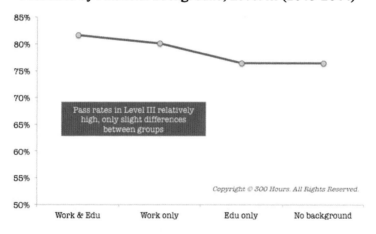

A similar pattern to Level I can be observed in Level III. Candidates with financial work experience consistently performed better than candidate groups without financial work experience.

Similar to Level I, financial education doesn't seem to be a significant factor in performance improvement.

However, the differences in pass rates between groups are now very small (about 5% compared to 10% in Level I), which again shows the high quality of candidates and intense competition in CFA Level III.

The least you need to know:

- *Financial work experience is consistently a strong contributing factor to performance across all levels*
- *Differences between groups start to diminish in Level III*

Financial work experience is consistently a strong contributing factor to performance across all levels.

Three important lessons from our financial background analysis

1. Just because you haven't any finance background doesn't mean you're hugely disadvantaged. Your drive and determination is an important asset in the CFA exams, and anyone can have.

2. A finance-related education doesn't necessarily equate to a better CFA exam performance, most likely due to complacency. The CFA exams are challenging, quite likely tougher than any exam you've had so far. Do not assume a background in finance will enable you to take it easy in your preparation.

3. Some CFA levels may suit you more than others. Depending on what you're best at and your contextual knowledge, you may find some CFA levels easier than others as the approach and content vary significantly, especially in Level III.

Just because you haven't any finance background doesn't mean you're hugely disadvantaged.

Section 7: How can candidates better address the Level III essay section?

Introduction

A very important success factor to passing Level III is performance in the constructed response session in the morning, also known as the 'essay format.

We reached out to the best performers in the Level III essay exam to gather their tips.

Besides being a completely new format to CFA candidates from Levels I and II, it is a session that candidates consistently perform poorly in. That is why this section specifically focuses on the essay session, and how to approach it effectively.

What is the 'essay' format?

What is referred to as the 'essay' question format is really a constructed response format in the morning paper. Questions are more open-ended and candidates are required to show workings for calculations and other reasonings.

This does not mean that questions have to be answered in the traditional essay sense. In fact, short bulleted answers work best - as long as the answers are the right ones!

Learn from the experts

In our analysis, we found out that an extremely high majority of candidates did poorly in the essay paper compared to their item-set paper – more than 80% of candidates in our sample performed worse in their essay session across the 2012 to 2014 exams.

We reach out to the best-performing candidates in the essay paper (i.e. those mostly scoring in the >70% bucket) and asked them for secrets to their successes. Several themes emerged quite clearly, and we present the findings in this section.

What you will learn in this section:

•   What are the main advice themes from successful candidates in the essay session

•   How to effectively prepare for the essay format

•   What traps to watch out for when answering essay questions

Lesson #1: Practice, practice, practice

Overwhelmingly, many responses stressed the importance of practice in some shape or form.

Even in the earlier levels of your CFA preparation, we've stressed on 300Hours.com the importance of practice exams to ensure familiarity with the scope and format of CFA questions. Level III is no exception, and with the new format it seems that practice is more important than ever.

> *Overwhelmingly, many responses stressed the importance of practice.*

This also correlates with our practice exam findings in Section 5 – Level III candidates attempt the most practice exams compared to other levels.

Here are what some of the top performers from the 2013 and 2014 Level III exams had to say about practicing and its contribution to their results.

- *"Practice the mocks until you are better at predicting what answers will get you the most points."*
- *"Do the CFAI supplied mock/sample exams repeatedly. Even though you'll get to know the questions inside out, you'll get to know the writing style they're looking for and it'll seep into the way you answer questions."*
- *"For the IPS questions, do not walk into the exam room without*

having solved at least 10 each (Individual and Institutional)."

- "I did 9 or 10 timed practice exams and for each one included an essay paper."

- "Even if I can't finish my revision in time, I will start doing my practice exams at least 1 month before exams. This is to let you know, from a "answering questions" perspective, what you are weak in and for you to focus more during your subsequent revisions."

- "... doing more practice papers is important this time because the essay questions are much more varied so any one paper is no longer as representative of what you may face on the exam as it was for L1/2."

- "I went through over a dozen essay practice exams ranging from old CFA tests and various 3rd party providers. I also went through these exams multiple times carefully grading them as well."

- "Between Schweser materials, CFA mocks, and prior year exams I ended up taking around 10 full (AM+PM) exams."

- "Study more than you think you need to... and then study some more after that."

Lesson #2: CFA Institute past-year exams are your best friends

Although CFA Institute does not release past papers for CFA Level I and II, they do have past papers for Level III essay questions, with corresponding model answers. This is usually downloadable in the 'example questions' part of the CFA Institute website.

You have to be utilizing this as much as you can. Past year papers are the closest representation of the real thing as you're going to get, and nothing is more uncertain than the essay format. At the very least you should be going through each and every past paper question and model answer before your own Level III exam.

> *"…doing all of the previous exams is the best way to learn the style in which CFA (Institute) wants answers."*

- *"One thing for certain though is (that) doing all of the previous exams is the best way to learn the style in which CFA wants answers."*
- *"I probably did each exam from 2007-2012 at least 5 times."*
- *"Just like any other CFA exam, the more practice papers you can do the better. It surprises me that some candidates don't look at the past exams the CFA Institute releases. I thought it was a given that you'd do that but I don't think everyone does."*
- *"Had saved up 5 years worth of prior (Level III) CFA exams by downloading all samples each year during Level I and II. Did one of*

those a week starting 7 weeks prior to exam."

- *"Practice cfa grey box multiple times. Do as many old am exams as possible."*
- *"Exam practice for the AM session is absolutely key. Do not ignore the past exams that the CFAI provides! Do them all, twice or three times, over the course of your study."*
- *"Do every single CFAI morning paper you can find."*

Lesson #3: Take and grade exams as realistically as possible

Questions in the essay section vary widely in length and points. The model answers also can be initially challenging to get used to, compared to the multiple choice answers you're used to from previous years.

Simulate exam conditions, timing and grading.

It's therefore super important for Level III candidates to especially make sure they complete their practice exams under as realistic exam conditions as possible.

Impose the exam conditions (no music or snacks), the right exam time limits, with no pausing the clock for breaks, and be strict with your grading after you've completed the practice exam.

Here are what some of the Level III performers had to say:

- *"Write your answer as if it was exam day."*
- *"Read the actual CFA material and take as many practice exams as possible in a timed setting."*
- *"Do lots of morning mock exams, under timed simulated exam conditions as much as possible."*
- *"When practicing, strictly stick with the given time limit per each individual question. No cheating or assume to steal time from other*

easier questions. If you can't solve it, then practice giving the best guess and move on."

- "Mark yourself very harshly on practice tests. If you have to think whether your answer fits the template answer, mark it wrong."

- "There is no better way to prepare (for the exam) than by actually writing AM papers under exam conditions."

- "Be conservative with grading, only give points when you hit exactly what they have in the rubric."

- "No cheating on self-grading; if not written out clearly, give zero points."

- "Do not underestimate the time pressure of the constructed response part of the exam. Organize your practice exams to mimic real exam like circumstances to gain confidence and routine in the pressures of the exam."

Lesson #4: Train to keep ahead of time

Sophie, one of the writers on our team, completed her CFA in 18 months straight. She was also one of the many candidates struggling for time in her Level III exam. For more details on her Level III experience, visit go.300hours.com/sophielevel3.

Time management is one of the key challenges in the Level III morning exam.

With the huge variation of points and unclear expected length of your answers, time management is definitely one of the key challenges in the Level III morning exam.

Some quick pointers:

- Always use short, to-the-point answers
- Use bullet points to quickly get your points across
- Use the number of points allocated to each question to roughly estimate how comprehensive your answer should be
- Check if the question includes an answer template – use it if it does!

Here are more tips, directly picked from Level III candidates' comments:

- *"Always use short sentences/bullets. One sentence per mark will suffice. Any more is time wasted. Always read the question; failure to read the question can result in wasted time."*
- *"The essay portion is the hardest. You are under significant time pressure, so you can't afford to spend more than the allocated time*

answering a question."

- "Focus on practicing the essay questions - they are not difficult material-wise but the small amount of time on the exam kills you."

- "There will be questions you can't answer. Move on, finish everything you know and come back."

- "It is imperative that you learn to do the individual and institutional IPS and required return calculations in a timely manner."

- "Answer to the point, work fast, use shortforms."

- "Running out of time seems to be the biggest problem for most of the people I talked to after the morning session. Keep track of time per question carefully during the actual exams. Since each question is given a different amount, many people I know skipped around many questions and lost track of how much time left vs. the remaining questions, not realizing that until the last 30 mins."

- "In the end, its not only about knowing the material, but putting it down in a quick and time saving manner. Aiming for perfection on exam day is a luxury few can afford. Taking too much time to write the perfect answer to get full credit in essay questions is not a good idea."

> "Answer to the point, work fast, use shortforms."

Lesson #5: Research the essay format questions and answer sheet thoroughly

The essay format will be new to you if you're taking Level III for the first time. So it's no surprise that the candidates that did best in it took the extra effort to research and understand the CFA essay format.

Familiarize yourself with the format early in your preparation. Make sure you understand how the answers work: some have a free-text field, while others may utilize a template or a table.

Make sure you identify the right answer template to be writing your answers in: candidates often mistake

> *"Look at the essay format before you do anything else for Level III."*

tables in the questions for answer templates and fill them up, but as it isn't in the answer template they receive zero points.

Speak to past candidates on how they found the format and what the challenges are, look through YouTube for videos explaining the CFA essay section. Many candidates recommended an instructional video by David Heatherington, which is free to access at go.300hours.com/level3video.

In essence, spend a little time researching the format, and it will go a long, long way.

- *"Understanding what you're up against is so crucial. Look at the essay format before you do anything else for Level III."*

83

- "...look when a template is being provided and make sure to use it."

- "Really get to grips with what the finished answer should look like - find some videos, talk to people who have passed, and if you can find a former marker of the exams (as I did), that's even better."

- "Start by writing down and labelling the relevant points from the text. Then I would clearly state what I was doing in terms of calculations, writing down the answers from each step. Finally, when I got to the answer, I would label it clearly, stating exactly what it was meant to show - from what I've heard, a lot just write down the starting information and then the answer. I was very careful to state exactly what each step was showing."

- "Keep answers very concise. Answer only what is asked. You don't need to complete sentences, phrases are fine."

- "For the most recent AM papers, pay close attention to what they asked and how it related to the content of the curriculum. Some of it was straight out of the book, while much of it was proper application of the curriculum."

We established a cut-off point for submissions several weeks after the results were released. Each annual sample size per level is about 2,000 to 3,000 unique, checked submissions.

How did you address duplicates and fake submissions?

A fundamental piece of how we decided to address duplicates and fakes was through a very simple mechanism - email addresses. If every submission included an email address we could very simply treat it as a unique identifier to spot 80% of duplicate cases, and fake email addresses automatically detected as fake entries. We also developed an algorithm to detect abnormal results. These are flagged for manual evaluation.

We use algorithms and manual inspection to weed out duplicates, fakes and bad submissions.

Once all this is done, we also inspected the entire sample manually to make sure the data is as clean as possible.

Where do I go to submit my result and obtain my personalized calculation?

Go to go.300hours.com/results to get your results breakdown. Using the same methodology for this analysis, we will calculate these scores and instantly get them to you:

- **Minimum theoretical score**: This is the minimum score possible for your level based on the results categories you scored in

- **Maximum theoretical score**: This is the maximum score possible for your level based on the results categories you scored in
- **40/60/80 score**: This is a purely assumed number, which assumes a mean score of 40% if you scored in the 0-50% category, 60% if you scored in 51%-70% category, and 80% if you scored in the 71%-100% category.

For more details on the theory behind these scores, see our "Getting Started" section.

How do you calculate the MPS of each level?

Since the theoretical maximum and minimum scores can be calculated for each result breakdown, given enough data around the Band 10 failures and passing score, a range of possibilities can be deduced, which becomes more accurate as the sample size increases.

Triangulating maximum, minimum and pass/fail grades of all qualified submissions gives us a range of possibilities where the MPS could lie. Given enough data points and enough performance difference between candidates, we then would be able to deduce the MPS value of each level.

For more details on methodology, see Section 3.

How sure are you that the MPS for each level is correct?

We're pretty sure, to be honest. We don't focus on this too much on 300Hours.com as CFA Institute frowns on making the MPS a key focal point.

We agree with CFA Institute on this – candidates should always aim to beat 70% when prepping. But as past candidates we also understand the curiosity around the MPS!

If we can take the assumption that the score categories (0-50%, 51%-70%, 71%-100%) are indeed exactly what CFA Institute say they are, then given enough samples the conclusion will be solid. The closer the difference between candidates, and the wider the individual minimum and maximum scores, the more challenging it is to deduce an exact number, which is why the range becomes pretty wide in Level III.

I compared maximum, minimum and 40/60/80 scores with my friend. We had similar scores, but yet one of us passed, and another failed. How is this possible?

The maximum, minimum and 40/60/80 scores, while good relative indicators, are obviously not your actual score. It's perfectly possible for two candidates to have exactly the same results breakdown (as provided by CFA Institute) and still have one that passed and another that failed, as there is a range of possible actual scores.

It would be interesting to see a breakdown by number of hours studied, or another idea I've thought of.

We were pretty strict this time on keeping the survey as short as possible (makes it easier for you!). We felt that 'number of hours studied' was too subjective a number (as it would be based on candidate recollection) to have any solid conclusions.

However, if you have a cool idea you want us to check out for next time, just email us at team@300hours.com!

Given the back and forth about Ethics - what is the conclusion? Should I or should I not focus on Ethics?

The answer to whether you should focus on Ethics is simple - yes! What the analysis is pointing out is that some candidates **overfocused** on Ethics - they score well in Ethics but everything else let them down. The lesson from this is to recognize when you've done enough on Ethics, and make sure you focus on the big topics for your particular level.

I failed. This is so frustrating...

It is frustrating. A few of us have experienced this, and the important thing is to use that experience to increase your drive to do better! It is not a great experience to not be handed a pass, and if you're feeling a bit lost, read more about what you can do at go.300hours.com/revenge.

My 40/60/80 score is higher than your stated MPS! I think I'm owed a pass.

Not necessarily. Your 40/60/80 score is based on pure theory and is not representative of your actual score. The MPS calculations, while solid in our opinion, is not acknowledged nor affiliated to CFA Institute. Please don't use this as a basis to argue for a pass. It won't work, and CFA Institute won't be pleased with us. Don't do it.

I have another question, or a suggestion.

Let us know at team@300hours.com, or drop by our Forum at

forum.300hours.com!

Printed in Great Britain
by Amazon